A Little Time to Rest . . . Eternally

Written by
HANNAH KARENA JONES

Illustrated by
JIMMY SIMPSON

PHILADELPHIA

RP Minis®
Hachette Book Group
1290 Avenue of the Americas, New York, NY 10104
www.runningpress.com
@Running_Press

First Edition: July 2026

Published by RP Minis, an imprint of Hachette Book Group, Inc. The RP Minis name and logo is a registered trademark of Hachette Book Group, Inc.

Contact specialmarkets@hbgusa.com regarding special discounts for bulk purchases.

The publisher is not responsible for websites (or their content) that are not owned by the publisher.

Design by Amanda Richmond

ISBN: 979-8-89414-179-4

Made in Dongguan, China (HKD) 03/26 #01

CONTENTS

GRAVEYARDS, THE PERFECT PLACE TO FIND YOUR ZEN

You are taking in a stroll through a quaint town just after supper. You turn a corner and stumble upon a seemingly long-forgotten cemetery, with headstones crumbling from centuries of wind and rain. Trees—now bare of leaves—creak ever so audibly in the light breeze, and a black cat darts out of a narrow space in the wrought-iron fence. Something about the graveyard draws you closer. You open the squeaky gate and are delighted to find a simple brick pathway leading to a solitary bench under a gnarled tree. You sit, arms gently resting in your lap, and close your eyes as the sun dips below the horizon. You hear . . . nothing—only the lulling noises of the night. This is a moment of Zen, of rest, that you least expected to find.

Graveyards are, by design, a setting for quiet contemplation. After all, they are supposed to be a peaceful place for the dead to rest for all eternity, as well as a safe and tranquil environment for their living loved ones to pay their respects.

Much like a Zen Garden, visiting is encouraged to have a quiet moment of reflection and introspection. It's also a time to connect deeply with one's ancestors and to channel an inner sense of tranquility. In your mini

Zen Garden Graveyard, these restorative powers blend and build on each other, offering a mental escape to somewhere as silent as the grave.

Yet, as the sun begins to set, beware that you don't trip over a crooked head-stone or fall six feet into a yet-unoccupied grave. After all, you want to be a visitor, not a resident.

GRAVEYARD RESIDENTS

Ghostly ladies, screaming skulls, glowing red eyes, statues that cry tears of blood, giggling children playing amid the tombstones, glowing orbs. These are all possible occurrences you might encounter on a spooky nighttime ghost tour of a graveyard as you search for your Zen.

On the surface, a graveyard may appear to be a simple collection of new and weathered headstones, marking lives once lived and now ended. But if you peer a little deeper as the sun sets and twilight draws near, you may suddenly find the fine hairs on your neck rise and goose bumps sprinkle across your arms. Try to embrace these sensations as a meditative moment—you just may be connecting with some lingering spirit who is wandering the cemetery, looking for worldly connection.

Of course, not all spectral graveyard residents are peaceful or passive. Some graveyards—particularly those with residents interred who have met ghastly ends or have committed heinous crimes—ooze a creepiness factor both day and night. Paranormal activity may abound, so you must choose your graveyard meditations wisely. Do your research for which graveyards have reports of malevolent spirits, devilish encounters, and unexplained spooky phenomena. If this is something that brings you Zen, excellent. If not, know that you'll be entering at your own risk.

GRAVEYARD AS GARDEN

Books and movies often portray graveyards as either creepy dwellings for undead creatures, like vampires and zombies, or as places of extreme grief and sadness. Yet graveyards are more than a place of supernatural happenings or deep mourning. In fact, many burial grounds are designated arboretums, such as the famous Laurel Hill Cemetery

in Philadelphia, which was founded in 1836. In addition to the 196,000 souls buried there, the cemetery is also home to more than 8,500 trees and shrubs, making it a peaceful, natural, and meditative spot for living visitors.

Laurel Hill Cemetery was established by John Jay Smith, a Quaker horticulturalist. Smith helped create the rural cemetery movement to combat the overcrowded, unsanitary, and aesthetically displeasing urban cemeteries. With Laurel Hill Cemetery, Smith and his colleagues aimed to provide a picturesque, airy, and landscaped environment for both burial and for those who wanted to reflect on life in a natural and inviting setting. Graveyards such as these are worth touring for their botanical merits alone, whether to admire the old-growth plantings, the colorful blooms, or the seasonal foliage display.

Landscaping a graveyard is also enhanced by hardscaping. *Hardscaping* refers to constructed elements that coincide with natural landscaped elements, such as walkways, benches, statues, fountains, walls, etc.

And for a graveyard, this also includes tombstones and mausoleums. These features are often constructed out of stone or concrete, and great care and attention to detail are provided by the artist to enhance the natural beauty of the cemetery landscape through ornamentation, statues, and intricate details engraved on these markers of remembrance. Next time you are in a graveyard, slow your pace and examine the beauty carved into these markers of eternal rest.

THE POWER OF GRAVEYARD DIRT

There is a long tradition of using graveyard dirt as a powerful ingredient in spells and other spiritual rituals. Dirt specifically sourced from a loved one's grave, for example, is considered well suited to a love spell.

It's important that the dirt is ethically gathered. Simply scurrying into a nearby graveyard under cover of darkness and stealing a scoop is a surefire way to offend a vengeful ghost or cause your spell to backfire. Instead, coordinate a respectful visit where you focus on asking for permission and honoring a sense of unease and displeasure if it arises—the dearly departed's way of rejecting the request. If, however, your gut says the spirit is giving the green light, offer a token of appreciation such as a flower arrangement, take no more than a handful of dirt, and thank the grave owner for sharing.

Alternatively, you can outsource the digging and

have it professionally procured. We guarantee that this synthetic purple graveyard dirt is 100 percent good vibes only and we *promise* it's not haunted (at least, not yet).

INTERACTING WITH YOUR ZEN GARDEN GRAVEYARD

If you are feeling overwhelmed by the daily grind—the overflowing email inbox, the unending social calendar, or the never-ending to-do list that requires you to zip all over town and never stop for a rest—take a quiet moment to pause and turn your attention to your tiny, peaceful Zen Garden Graveyard. Imagine taking a serene, solo walk through a real cemetery, feeling a brisk autumn breeze and resting against a weathered headstone.

Using your ethically sourced graveyard dirt, follow traditional

Zen gardening techniques to yield calming benefits. Clear your mind as you pour the graveyard dirt into the tray. In addition to the purple dirt, you've been provided with everything you need for a peaceful moment of Zen: a withered, spooky tree; mini headstones; skeleton bones; a gravedigger's shovel; and a black cat.

Gathering your items, you can now focus on arranging

them in a pleasing display. Root your timeworn tree. Carefully place each headstone, perhaps offering a prayer for each spirit they represent. Perform a respectful burial ritual, returning the skeleton's bones to the Earth and covering them with the soil. Use your shovel to smooth out the graves and place the cat nearby to keep watch. Meander through the mini-scenic sanctuary you've created and take time to reflect.

Perhaps you need something spookier to settle your soul. Wait until after dark, when the leafless tree starts casting eerie shadows, the gnarled branches looming and grasping like monster claws. A black cat might slink out and cross your path at any moment, hissing and arching its back as a warning to beware of the unseen spirits in the night. You use the shovel to gleefully dig graves for your enemies or perhaps to dig up a collection of bones and put them on unsettling and prominent display. Perhaps in your graveyard, artfully scattering those bones from one corner to the other is the best method to achieve a sense of Zen.